LIVING THE 10+ PLUS LIFE

PRAISE FOR
Living the 10+ Life

"Kim Somers Egelsee is back with a book filled with easy to apply tips and tools for keeping your life at an extraordinary level. *Living the 10+ Life* is a must read for anyone wanting extra confidence in their life."

JEANETTE ORTEGA
Extreme Results Fitness and Author of
The Little Black Book of Fitness

"Kim Somers Egelsee has had a tremendous impact on my life and my progress - in who I want to be and how I want to be truly living. Her 10+ approach is so practical, effective and holistic that it has definitely propelled me to the next level of joy, fulfillment, and massive action into the confident creative me I am ready to be. Kim has such unique, inspiring, effective approaches, and her custom designed exercises, tips and strategies are really potent and powerful for clearing out what is stopping us and helping us to finally move into how we can really share our gifts with the world. *Living the 10+ Life* is a perfect way to jumpstart your self-love and self-growth practices, as well as help you to actualize a life where you are feeling connected and impassioned about the life you are creating and leading."

LAURA JANE
Yoga Muse and Author of *Feel Better NOW*

"*Living the 10+ Life* made me feel a sense of enlightenment, that we are not born superstars but we build on our experiences and layering process of ourselves, to become who we are. Life is a journey and not a destination, and we make choices in our lives that lead us to different roads. Remarkable!"

XIOMARA ESCOBAR
Beauty Ambassador

"As a friend and admirer of Kim Somers Egelsee for years, I have seen first hand how she has created a 10+ life for herself and others lucky enough to learn from her. Her first book, *Getting Your Life to a 10 Plus*, was an amazing book filled with wisdom and actionable tips. Her new book *Living the Ten+ Life* has even more tips, tools and wisdom that will allow you to start living your 10+ life right now."

MONICK PAUL HALM
Founder of Real Estate Investor Goddesses and
Author of *The Inner Game*

"In *Living the 10+ Life*, Kim Somers Egelsee delivers superb coaching on how you can achieve your full potential. Her expertise, with many years as a life and business coach, are brilliantly unraveled in these pages. I have had the great fortune to be in many of Kim's programs and have used the tools offered in this book to get my life to a 10+!"

JACKIE VANCAMPEN
Wise Heart Within and Bestselling Author

"Throughout the years, Kim Somers Egelsee has shown her compassion and expertise in her arena from getting on stage and speaking life into her audiences, and through her interaction with the people close to her, always leaving them a gem of confidence in every conversation."

RASHEED LOUIS
Epiphany Marketing

"*Living the 10+ Life* is the ideal book for anyone who wants to increase their confidence and live a magical life! Kim Somers Egelsee will inspire you to take chances, express yourself and live boldly."

DANIELLE AUGUSTIN
Blowtini Blow Out Bar

LIVING THE 10+ PLUS LIFE

Affirmations, Tips and Activities for Increased Confidence and Success

KIM SOMERS EGELSEE

GET BRANDED PRESS

Copyright © 2017 Kim Somers Egelsee

All rights reserved.
No portion of this book may be reproduced mechanically, electronically, or by any other means, including photocopying, without written permission of the publisher. It is illegal to copy this book, post it to a website, or distribute it by any other means without permission from the publisher.

Get Branded Press
Newport Beach, CA 92663
www.GetBrandedPress.com

Limits of Liability and Disclaimer of Warranty.
The author and publisher shall not be liable for your misuse of this material. This book is strictly for informational and educational purposes.

Warning – Disclaimer.
The purpose of this book is to educate and entertain. The author and/or publisher do not guarantee that anyone following these techniques, suggestions, tips, ideas, or strategies will become successful. The author and/or publisher shall have neither liability nor responsibility to anyone with respect to anyone with respect to any loss or damage caused, or alleged to be caused, directly or indirectly by the information contained in this book.

ISBN 978-1-944807-02-3 paperback
ISBN 978-1-944807-03-0 ebook
Library of Congress Cataloging-in-Publishing Data is available upon request.

Printed in the United States of America
First Printing, 2017

Edited by Taylor Augustin www.GetBrandedPress.com
Cover & Interior Design by Kate Korniienko-Heidtman
Back Cover Photography by Rasheed Louis

I dedicate this book to my daughters Nia and Noella.
You inspire, uplift and motivate me to
follow my dreams and create magic daily!

ACKNOWLEDGMENTS

Huge gratitude to my supportive, loving and amazing husband Edwin, my parents who are also my best friends, and Susie Augustin who is my partner in crime and just gets me. I am so thankful for her hard work and dedication.

Gratitude shout-outs to Kyle Wilson for being my mentor, Niurka for huge transformation, Robin Duncan for spiritual healing and wisdom, Eden Sustin for life changing communication, Doris Muna for wisdom, Prince for being my glowing inspiration, and to my mastermind sisters who truly support, uplift and encourage me so much.

TABLE OF CONTENTS

FOREWORD *by Susie Augustin*	**10**
INTRODUCTION	**12**
CHAPTER ONE **10+ CONFIDENCE**	15
CHAPTER TWO **10+ CONNECTIONS**	39
CHAPTER THREE **10+ CORE**	51
CHAPTER FOUR **10+ COURAGE**	63
CHAPTER FIVE **10+ CREATIVE EXPRESSION**	83
CHAPTER SIX **10+ CONSCIOUSNESS**	95
CHAPTER SEVEN **10+ COMMUNICATION, CHOICES & CREATIONS**	109
ABOUT KIM SOMERS EGELSEE	129

FOREWORD

Are you ready to exude confidence in every aspect of your life? *Living the 10+ Life* provides you with the tips and tools to empower you to create opportunities and take action to transform your life. Kim Somers Egelsee shares stories of her life when she was not living in her full positive power, what led to her insecurities, and what she did to pull herself out of self-doubt and feeling like she wasn't enough. She attended personal development seminars and studied extensively, read books just like the one you're reading now, which taught her how to banish negative talk and behavior, embrace her uniqueness and talents, and connect with others in a very powerful way. She took charge and learned how to live the life of her dreams, and she wants everyone to know how to make impactful changes to live a life filled with confidence and happiness.

I've always felt I had an abundance of confidence, I embraced my creativity since I was young, and I pursued acting and anything beauty-related for many years. But just like many of you, when I got older and entered the workforce, I had challenges with others who wanted me to dull my sparkle and conform to their standards. I met Kim during a time of such challenges, and she helped me stay centered and in my power, while I was required to perform at very high standards with unrealistic expectations.

Knowing that I'm a marketing copywriter in the beauty industry, Kim asked me to edit the manuscript for her first book, *Getting Your Life to a 10 Plus*. She also asked me to speak at her monthly Willow Tree Women's Circle on the topic Health, Beauty and Sex Appeal. Developing material for my presentation made me delve deep into what beliefs I held about confidence, beauty and what it means to be sexy. After my talk, many women asked me if I would write a book on the topic, and a year later I wrote *Sexy, Fit & Fab at Any Age!* Kim and I collaborated on our books and planned on having a red carpet book launch together, inspiring me to publish both of our books and start my own publishing imprint Get Branded Press. Both books have won awards and are Amazon bestsellers.

Kim is such an amazing and supportive person, friend and coach, and she has the ability to see unique talents in others that they sometimes don't even see in themselves. We've done events together, and her talent to connect with people and develop a loyal following are so impressive. She wants everyone to live a *10+ Life* and encourages us to follow our passions. Together with Rasheed Louis, we created Passion Power Confidence web series, which can be viewed on YouTube.

Having Kim in my life as my friend, accountability partner and inspiration has definitely changed my life in a positive way. Her encouragement led me to know my worth, no longer let anyone dull my sparkle, and start my brand and series of *Sexy, Fit & Fab* books. What will this book inspire in you? We'd love to hear about your stories of success when you dare to live a 10+ Life!

Live the live of your dreams and follow your passion!

SUSIE AUGUSTIN is the bestselling author of *Sexy, Fit & Fab at Any Age!*, *Sexy, Fit & Fab Sirens*, and upcoming *Sexy, Fit & Fab Beauty Secrets*. Her writing, speaking and publishing have garnered her awards and nominations. She is a Beauty & Branding Expert and has worked with some of the world's top rated beauty companies. Susie is committed to helping women increase their self-confidence and improve their body image through exploring their inner and outer beauty, inspiring them to develop their essences, exude confidence, embrace their true selves and feel extraordinary. To help others pursue their dreams and brand themselves through their writing, Susie wrote *Writing to Wow! Book Writing Workbook* and created Get Branded Press, offering editing, ghostwriting and publishing. Her mission is ***Dream it. Write it. Brand it.***

www.SexyFitFab.com

INTRODUCTION

Go from being a glimmer of light to a beam of shining brightness! Let out who you are and radiate it out to change the world.

It's never too late to achieve, grow and become! You can begin to bloom today!

Up until I was a young adult, I never won awards and was always the last to get chosen on the playground. I didn't get recognition and felt I wasn't truly exceptional at any one thing. I just saw that I was somewhat good at a couple of things and accepted that's how it would always be. It used to make me fairly sad, but I still continued to study, work on myself and move forward.

In my twenties I worked as a waitress while chasing an acting career. I worked as a model, actor, movie and television extra, host, sang backup in a rock group, did some producing, public relations, marketing and more. I worked in the field of special education and felt very good about that, but still didn't think I had met my full potential.

I had several periods in my life when I hit bottom and climbed my way out. I met and worked with different mentors and sifted through several friendships, making sure they were positive influences.

I remained positive by believing in myself and dedicated my time to stepping into my life's true purpose. I had spent over 20 years studying Jim Rohn, Og Mandino and other personal development greats. I had my college degree, credentials and experience, and with the encouragement of several mentors, I began life coaching on the side. As I remained open to my purpose soaring in, I started studying with a transformational teacher named Niurka, getting certified in NLP and Supreme Influence. I had a huge breakthrough and realized that teaching others to live extraordinary lives was my objective. Through this, I met Nung Rigor who encouraged me to begin inspirational speaking. I woke up one day realizing and knowing I was 100% in my passion and purpose…and it was spectacular. I spoke at events, coached people, and refined my speaking by saying yes to many exciting occasions. Craving practice, I asked for chances to speak, creating my own opportunities and jumping into them. This included hosting and leading over 400 workshops, meetings and events in over seven years.

Due to the passion and urgency I felt during that time in my life, it all paid off by shifting my life to an extra fulfilling level. I have won ten awards in the last few years for my connecting, writing, coaching and speaking, which is a far cry from my childhood where I won nothing. I accomplished a prestigious Tedx talk, co-hosted an international show, and wrote a number one bestselling book, *Getting Your Life to a 10 Plus: Finding Your Purpose, Being in Your Power and Living an Amazing Life.* I created several amazing courses with Kyle Wilson, the man behind the top personal development mentors including Og Mandino, Zig Zigler and Brian Tracey, who are a big influences on my life.

Kyle was Jim Rohn's 18 year partner and the founder of Jim Rohn International, and he helped me produce my 10+ Life Coach Certification and Confidence Course. I have shared stages with the greats such as Brian Tracy and Darren Hardy. Additionally, I led my own 10+ mastermind groups. I am constantly speaking, coaching and writing aligned with my life's purpose. This has been a lifelong buildup of knowledge, experiences, wisdom, mistakes, study and successes. Within the last four years my purpose and passion was born, fueled and is still flying high.

This book is the sequel to my first book. It is designed to be a go-to manual for keeping yourself fueled with positivity, motivation and empowerment at all times. I hope you will use both books as your resources for 10+ greatness. Go for your dreams. Stay strong in your belief in yourself and your visions. Believe you will get there, and you will go far.

CHAPTER ONE

10+
CONFIDENCE

5 STEPS TO BOOST CONFIDENCE

Confidence is being in tune with your truest self, dreams and purpose. When you design your life and career plans exactly as your heart desires, exuding your authentic self in every interaction, innovative planning, marketing and social media success are effortless. Creating your own magical opportunities is possible by connecting with powerful positive people, clearing yourself of baggage and fear, staying balanced and in the flow, and looking at life as an adventure!

1. Be you. Have the nerve to hold nothing back. Start to check in with yourself to be sure you aren't people pleasing, hiding, criticizing or downplaying who you truly are. Start by appreciating yourself and your gifts, talents and attributes. Make sure to acknowledge the great things you've accomplished throughout your life. Remember to accept you for who you are. Of course it's wonderful to want to grow, shift and change, but acceptance first is key.

2. Live opened up to love, light, unlimited possibilities, people and the beauty of the world. Remain receptive by understanding you can learn from everyone you meet. Be optimistic that your life is and can be extraordinary.

3. Create your own opportunities and jump into them. Don't wait for that project or job to appear. Start with small daily steps to attain what you dream of. Ask for help and connections. Ask for chances and big things. Be bold. Take risks. For some, this may mean trying a new food, while for others it may be taking on a new sport, exercise or project.

4 Sort through everything you are doing now in your life and rate each item 0-100%: 100 makes you feel on fire, fueled and fulfilled. Get rid of the things that aren't at least 90% to make the space for greatness, rewards and your dreams to come into your life. Next, start to shape and sculpt your life by design. What are your dreams, and are you on your way to achieve them?

5 Talk to yourself and others positively. Throw away any negative thoughts about yourself. Treat yourself like a star, and others will too.

What magical opportunities are you creating?

SELF CONFIDENCE STRENGTHENING MEDITATION

This is a guided meditation that you can use for yourself or others for more self-love, self-appreciation and positive power. Be sure to take three deep and cleansing breaths before starting. Breathe in serenity and breathe out any low energy.

I want you to now visualize yourself sitting, relaxed in a gorgeous serene location. You feel flowing and at ease in every way. As you see yourself in this beauty, you also feel amazing, look remarkable and have your favorite things surrounding you, such as photos, flowers, items and objects that hold significance.

As you sit in this beauty, you see a bright, shining and radiant blue light surrounding you. It starts to sweep over and within your whole body. This light magically and powerfully cleanses away any negativity within you about yourself, your life, your abilities and talents. It fills in the knowingness and certainty that you have power, confidence, talents, abilities, positivity and self-esteem. You are filled with self-acceptance, self-appreciation, self-love, self-awareness and self-esteem. You are overflowing positive and powerful self-love, self-appreciation, self-awareness and self-esteem. This blue light emotionally uplifts, encourages and supports you.

Physically, feel the warmth of this blue magnificent light around and within you and your being. Feel the love it brings. It cleanses away all negativity, doubt, insecurities and uncertainties. It leaves the power within so that you will always, from this point on, have powerful and fulfilling confidence and self-esteem. This power the blue light is leaving with you will give you continuous certainty, positive power and confidence. Anytime you need this extra confidence boost, feel the warmth of the blue light within.

You realize now that your self-love and confidence have always been there in its fullness. The blue light just cleansed away some of the blocks. This self-love and acceptance becomes more powerful daily. You love yourself and others and this radiates from your being naturally from now on. Positive people and opportunities now flow to you easily and effortlessly. You know and have certainty about your talents and abilities. You are able to help others more freely with this new power and confidence. You look forward to every day because you now have your full and positive power flowing from you, radiating and attracting positivity. You look, feel and are Greatness! Confidence! Power! Love!

FEEDBACK IS ONE WAY TO CONFIDENCE!

How to Ask For and Receive Feedback That can Change Your Life.

Feedback is something that can magnify your life and increase your success, actions and attitude. It is a way for you to see yourself from others' perspectives. People can often become confused as to what they truly want to do in their life, what their purpose may be or if they should follow their passions and heart's desire. Asking for feedback can give you so many answers. Start today. Choose eight people that you know. It can be a combination of those you work with, friends, people on social media and family. Send an email letting them know that you are doing a project from an article that you read and would love for them to answer three questions:

1. How do you see me? Describe in several words.
2. What are my talents and gifts?
3. What are some constructive criticisms you can give me?

When you receive the results, you will most likely be happily surprised and have a major confidence boost. (Just the bravery of doing this exercise boosts your confidence). You will now discover some talents that you didn't realize that you had, traits that you can bring out even more now that you know people see you that way, a few things that you can improve and some new career or project ideas. Now that you see your life in a different light, your confidence will continue to build.

Finally, create a list of 10-50 things you love about you. Take this information and create a plan. Find three words that describe you best and keep those in the back of your mind. Brainstorm new passions. Decide which traits you will emphasize and use and watch your self-esteem boost to higher plains. To think that we know how others see us can be delusional. If we constantly wonder what others think of us, it can cause uncertainty and unease, which can show in our demeanor and energy. It is extremely powerful to dare and ask others how they see you. What constructive criticisms can they give you? What talents do they think you have? Enjoy this process and see your confidence, self-esteem and life soar!

LIVING IN YOUR FULL POSITIVE POWER

Living in your full positive power means following your passions and taking actions on your dreams and what's in your heart, not for others but for yourself. This means having spunk, spirit and enthusiasm about life and yourself. It means being savvy, having the intelligence to ask for help, and paying attention to your inner scale with integrity when making decisions. It means being open minded, full of integrity and optimism and having the nerve to be you. It is exuding confidence in any interaction, moving forward fearlessly, being bold, believing in yourself and thinking creatively outside of the box. Most importantly it is spending time with positive people.

You feel this power all throughout your body and your soul. It helps you make decisions. It helps you take action. It helps you love yourself. It makes you extraordinary overall. I live this way now and it's amazing, fun and magical, all while making life much easier. Even when hardships or problems arise, I'm able to handle them much better.

But it wasn't always this way. I had several experiences where I almost gave up my power for good. When I was nine years old I had a lot of friends in the neighborhood that I played with. I was a leader, coordinating shows with all of the kids, having meetings in the clubhouse my grandpa made for me, and creating games for the kids to play.

One girl that we hung out with was pretty mean, had an attitude problem and got her power from being a bully to others. She was one of those people who chased and created drama. Of course I thought hanging out with her was exciting and made me also feel kind of powerful and rebellious, which is exciting when you're a kid. We would do crazy things like break eggs in people's mailboxes and play ding dong ditch.

Coming from my normal family and home where I was an only child and had a lot of stability, I felt excited being with her, even though I had a strange feeling inside me that my behavior was poor and I was not making good choices. Finally, like all dramatic and rebellious people, the relationship took a turn one day when this so-called friend went from being sweet and fun with me, to turning on me in a very mean way when she said, "Don't you know no one likes you anymore?" She began spreading rumors about me that were untrue and made up stories about what I was saying and doing around our community. This caused all of the kids in the neighborhood to turn their back on me and abandon me. I went home crushed, crying and feeling completely abandoned and alone.

When I was 11 and in the sixth grade, another incident at school happened. The boys in my class had the girls line up in a row and they rated how pretty we were by lining us up in order of how good looking we were. They went girl by girl and ended up choosing me as one of the last girls, which basically meant that they thought I was ugly. I felt a lump in my throat, like I wanted to run away and go home. Instead, I put on a brave face and sucked in my tears.

These are just two of the many times as a child and teenager where I lost my full power. I let my positive power be taken away. Instead of dealing with how I felt, I kept it to myself and became a people pleaser, hanging onto friends and doing what made them happy, so I wouldn't have to ever lose a bunch of friends again. I went above and beyond trying to look beautiful and started wearing make up at age 12, coloring my hair at age 13, and dressing overly sexy. The attention I received made me feel pretty and admired. Little did I know that this type of behavior was a result of the self-esteem destroying incidents that I had never dealt with.

I was living to please others and was not following my heart. I went on like this until age 19. I began dating a very popular guy I had a huge crush on all throughout high school. He was good-looking, cool, and I had even named my goldfish after him in the past.

I was so thrilled that he liked me, so I jumped into a relationship with him. Very quickly there were warning signs that I had made a big mistake. He was extremely jealous, started to get incredibly mean over small things, and even became verbally abusive by calling me horrible names. He was also a very obvious compulsive liar. *What was I doing?* I put up with it and made excuses for him. At one point I created a chart of the total number of days we didn't fight. I wouldn't listen to friends and family members that told me to dump him. I began to feel sad and negative more often and it definitely began affecting my confidence.

I started to feel the very opposite of the powerful positive person that I truly was. I felt powerless and stupid for even being involved in this situation; but little did I realize, it had become my project. I was trying to fix him.

One night, when we went out for my birthday, a guy flirted with me at a restaurant. My boyfriend got so angry with me that he actually hit me; I ended up jumping out of our car while it was moving. Enough was enough. But I still didn't learn and just kept on trying to fix and change him, until I noticed that he had a gambling problem. We had been saving money to take a vacation to Mexico together, and he ended up gambling all of the money away, including all of my money that I had saved for months.

One night we got into such a dramatic fight that we began screaming and throwing things at each other, and the neighbors called the police on us. The two policemen banged on the door and threatened to arrest us if we didn't stop. I felt shocked. *How did I get myself into such a dysfunctional mess? Was I addicted to the drama or trying to fix someone?* It all went downhill from there. I was so done with the relationship but each time I tried to leave, he would threaten to kill himself. Finally, I just couldn't take it. I wasn't responsible for his actions and behavior. I wanted my sweet and happy powerful self back, so I left him. For GOOD!

How did I change? First of all, I came into realization and acceptance of what was really happening. I reflected on the fact that I had been trying to fix him; this played a huge factor in what caused this.

We are all born with our positive, strong and pure power. Little by little things happen to hide this power and we must dig deep to find it. We must shed layers. He had become my project. However, by really evaluating my life, I realized the positive power of CHOICE and reflected on the choices I was making. *Who was I spending my time with? What was I doing? Where was I directing my energy?* No one had been forcing me to spend time or chunks of my life with these people from my past.

Then, deciding in little steps to make positive changes in my life, I went to see a famous personal development self-help success speaker named Jim Rohn, from who I learned about setting goals and "working harder on yourself than you do on your job". I began reading more books including *Think and Grow Rich* by Napoleon Hill and *The Game Of Life And How To Play It* by Florence Scovel Shinn.

I weeded my garden of friends and slowly began hanging out less with drama creators and more with positive and creative people full of kindness and compassion. I began regularly reading positive books, working toward my dreams and doing volunteer work. Instead of trying to fix others, I was truly making a difference in the world.

My life began to change pretty rapidly for the better, and I began to have more and more positive power. It began to naturally flow in and out of me. I met the guy of my dreams and am now happily married with two girls, a house by the beach and an amazing career where I get to uplift, encourage and help others. Now every day I get to practice living in my full positive power in all aspects of my life!

3 MAIN TIPS AND TOOLS TO LIVE IN YOUR FULL POWER

1. Choose positive people to hang out with; you are who you hang out with. In turn, your new power will bless so many and give them permission to have power too. Focus on helping others find their power. Surround yourself with people who "SUE" you: Support, Uplift and Encourage you, and you them.

2. Try new projects and bold out-of-your-comfort-zone goals. Prove to yourself that you can do it, and then celebrate your accomplishments. Each time you'll go further with your success.

3. Change your communication. Reframe negative words into positive ones and watch your life soar. For example, instead of saying you are anxious, you are *anticipating amazing things*. Instead of being stressed, you are simply *challenging yourself to be even greater*.

Finally, try something powerful. Take a deep breath, close your eyes and let it out. Now I want you to remember a time when you were unstoppable, you felt amazing with either something you achieved or a project you were working on or an event you were a part of. Take a minute to really see that.

Think of a time when you were filled with boundless energy, enthusiasm and confidence. Experience how you were feeling, hear the sounds around you, really be in your body and celebrate. Now amp that feeling up a notch and be in it! Make it big, bright, amazing, bold, brave, fearless and courageous. Now take a deep breath to breathe in this feeling and open your eyes.

If you could envision this, you can have it all. Fear is denying yourself permission to have it all. Stop making excuses and start making choices. Now I want you to close your eyes again and this time visualize a time in the future where you will be in your full positive power. See yourself being on fire, confident, taking action on your dreams. You have this inside of you. Bring it out and celebrate you!

List a new way you will let out your positive power from now on.

AMP UP YOUR CONFIDENCE TODAY

Do something bold to amp up your confidence! Train your mind to shift into new possibilities. Here are some tips and activities to add courage and bold energy.

1. Take a course
2. Meet with an uplifting mentor
3. Read something powerful and inspiring
4. Write an article
5. Create a new project
6. Speak in public
7. Volunteer
8. Wear red all week long
9. Try out false eyelashes (a note mostly for the ladies)
10. Work with an image consultant to amp up your style
11. Add highlights to your hair
12. Walk like a supermodel
13. Try out acrylic nails a bit longer than you ever have
14. Take an acting, improv or voice class
15. Attend an event or networking meeting that's new and unfamiliar

10 DAY CONFIDENCE CHALLENGE

Burst through to your most confident self by participating in this 10 Day Confidence Challenge. Each day, complete one bold task and post your results to share with your social media peers. This will ensure that you hold yourself accountable. Challenge one new friend to the challenge each day. At the close of the ten days, you will feel a huge increase in courage, confidence and bold energy. Let's do it!

DAY 1: Talk to five strangers and compliment them on something with a big smile.

DAY 2: Take a selfie of you "owning it" and post on social media with "I am amazing" as the title.

DAY 3: Post ten things you love about yourself.

DAY 4: Make two phone calls asking for something that you would normally be fearful of asking for.

DAY 5: Walk like you are a star with your head held high; make eye contact with people you encounter and smile.

DAY 6: Publicly declare to everyone you know a bold dream, vision or goal.

DAY 7: Wear something red, bold, hot, confident and smashing!

DAY 8: Push yourself physically by hiking, running, roller skating or dancing. Kick up the endorphins.

DAY 9: Use only positive and empowering words today. No Complaining.

DAY 10: Send a message to ten people telling them they are extra awesome.

How did you do each day? What did you learn?

Make notes here:

_____
_____
_____
_____
_____
_____
_____
_____
_____
_____
_____
_____
_____
_____
_____
_____
_____

10 SECRETS TO A CONFIDENT LOVE RELATIONSHIP

1. Make sure to participate in positive and regular communication. Know what makes one another fulfilled and happy.

2. Have a knowing for one another's intentions. For example, Frank's intention for his relationship with Deborah is to always show love, compassion and trust. This way when there is a miscommunication, Deborah knows that Frank's intentions are not to hurt or betray her.

3. Grow together. Read some of the same books, have deep talks, attend seminars, start a project, make a vision board, travel and share memories.

4. Schedule in fun. Keep doing the same exciting adventures that brought you together in the first place. Have good stress such as working out together, hiking, trying a new restaurant, going to a concert or magic show.

5. Keep up the intimacy; find out what you and your partner need. See how they communicate. Maybe she needs to see you dressed up. Maybe he loves to hear nice compliments. Maybe she is happy with extra hugs and kisses.

6. Be comfortable and confident with separate activities and projects and be confident and excited to be in tune and aligned together, too.

7 Love yourself and your partner. Make sure you can both have a list of the things you love about one another.

8 Share values, compromise, experience one another's interests.

9 Laugh as often as possible!

10 See the greatness in one another, respect, support, uplift and encourage each other.

What are some of the ways you can enhance your relationship?

_____
_____
_____
_____
_____
_____
_____
_____
_____
_____
_____
_____
_____
_____
_____
_____

4 WAYS TO SHINE CONFIDENTLY IN YOUR FIELD

1. Stand Out!

Standing out means to confidently show up and walk your talk. Be exceptionally good; do more than you're paid for or more than expected. Have extreme integrity, be authentic and reveal your unique qualities without fear.

2. Be an Influencer!

Being an influencer means to be known for being great, successful or an expert at something; to inspire, help others to succeed with passion, kindness and generosity. Being an influencer is to speak, write and teach on your wisdom.

3. Engage and Express!

Engaging and expressing yourself means to talk with people both live and online while being a great listener. It is to express your gifts, talents, knowledge and emotions with ease, excitement and eloquence.

4. Be Bold!

Being bold means to shine in ways that match your personality and vision. Such as wearing a bold dress or suit, wild shoes, speaking up for what you believe in and saying "no" to anything that you're not 100% excited about. Being bold means saying "yes" to challenging projects that will stretch you, make you stronger and more of an expert at what you do.

TIPS FOR CONFIDENT SEX APPEAL

Gorgeous, glamorous, fancy, sassy, sexy, chic and beautiful! Do things to make yourself look and feel this way as much as you can and you'll feel happier celebrating yourself.

- **S** – Study you; what makes you feel confident and sexy?
- **E** – Exude enthusiasm and excitement about your life.
- **X** – XOXO. Love yourself and love people; have the belief that you are worth knowing.
- **A** – Accept yourself: body, personality and life so far. We are all a work in progress. You must accept first and make changes after.
- **P** – Practice; act as if you are as sexy as you can imagine.
- **P** – Positive; make the most of your positive attributes and attitude.
- **E** – Embrace your appearance.
- **A** – Adjust; what can you grow on, change or repair?
- **L** – Laughter is so attractive.

List what makes you feel sexy here:

List what you can start to do to amp up your sex appeal and feel fabulous here:

8 KEYS TO SEXY
by Susie Augustin

Uncover the 8 Keys to being *Sexy, Fit & Fab at Any Age!*

Explore your inner beauty, develop your essence, embrace your true self and feel extraordinary while you experience your confidence increasing.

Anyone can have it all. Are your ready?

The first key is Spirit – exploring faith, gratitude and inspiration.
The second key is Nutrition – enjoying whole foods, hydration, and support.
The third key is Exercise – getting physically fit, active and being in nature.
The fourth key is Education – earn a degree, read books and use your brain.
The fifth key is Passion – follow your passion or purpose, career and hobbies.
The sixth key is Personality – embracing your uniqueness, having a positive attitude, and a sense of humor.
The seventh key is Grooming – personal appearance including skin, hair, makeup, clothes and fashion.
The eighth key is Sex Appeal – confidence, inner beauty and balance, and having passion for life.

Prepare yourself for transformation. Learn how to make the most of your assets and discover your beauty from the inside out. Imagine the life you can have when you have vision and follow your passion. When you are self-assured, have faith, feel strong, and are happy, you'll exude a natural spark, which is very attractive and alluring. You'll become magnetic and draw others to you. What you radiate out you will get in return.

Exude your confidence and *Keep it Sexy!*

10+ CONFIDENCE TIPS & AFFIRMATIONS

Confidence is when you decide to, get to, can, know and own your power.

Confidence is when you no longer *should, have to, can't or aren't good enough to.*

Confidence is taking positive, bold actions and to be who you are destined to be.

There are opportunities daily in everything; look for them always. The more confidence you learn, build, create and step into, the bigger, better and more positive opportunities come to you. Form your own thoughts, create your own power and jump into your opportunities that you create. You CAN do this!

Snails, clams and turtles have shells, not humans! Take yours off and let go. Have the nerve to be you. Don't you think it's time to step into your power and stand out in order to exude your greatness? Stand out from the crowd, dare to go for your best, jump into greatness. Get to that shining place of confidence where you unapologetically own it!

Spirit Tip: Tune into your heart, the air, the energy, vibes, earth and your soul and make decisions and create ideas that way.

Set your old self free and tune into your true self, letting it soar! Dare to act, behave and be extremely confident; exude knowingness and certainty.

Start questioning why you feel you cannot do something or why you feel you should do something. Are either of these facts, or just beliefs you've decided? Self-love means to work on your true self, know the true you and be aware of what choices you are making moment by moment.

With age, every year gains you greater confidence, wisdom, knowing, sexiness, poise, grace, acceptance and appreciation.

Exude inner-peace, outer-confidence and love. Get to a place in your life where you almost always have only smiles, positive thoughts, full confidence, inner-power, peace, love and success; yes, it really is possible: what's your next step to get there?

Today I dare you to spread confidence by seeing someone's power or beauty and letting him or her know. Realize that who you are starts with an inner knowing of power and confidence that you're already amazing and that you can radiate it out to the world.

Position yourself as an expert. If you don't believe in you, no one else can. Have confidence. Play Big, Bigger, Biggest!

Be BOLD! What's one huge daring power goal you have for yourself? Declare it here:

_____
_____
_____
_____
_____
_____
_____
_____
_____
_____
_____
_____
_____
_____
_____
_____

CHAPTER TWO

10+
CONNECTIONS

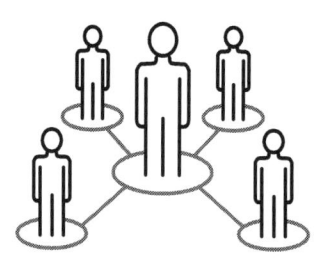

CONNECT WITH THOSE WHO SUE YOU – SUPPORT, UPLIFT AND ENCOURAGE YOU

Choose positive people to hang out with and you will have power. You are who you hang out with and in turn your new power will bless so many and give them permission to have power too. Remember that connecting with someone can lead to friendship, referrals, support, feedback, an accountability partner, a family-like closeness and being uplifted. Additionally, they may see something amazing in you that you don't see in yourself! Make a new connection today.

Work to find the good in everyone you encounter.

Be present to other's true hearts and real selves shining through any walls and layers they may have. You seeing that in them will help them see it themselves.

Spread kindness to others today. Give extra smiles, hugs and positive feedback. You never know whom you will touch and it just might be yourself.

Spend time working on positive communication and life will get much easier and more joyful.

The energy of being involved in a mastermind, workshop, seminar or retreat with positive people creating growth and change is an extraordinary shift for all involved. We all have much more in common than we realize. We all need love and connection. We have powerful energy and intuition. We all have empathy, strength, compassion and more. When we can come together for deeper connection, communication, thought and learning, it is even more special. We can see deeply into one another's souls and truly connect and support one another.

What will you do to begin connecting more? Will you join a mastermind group, attend more events and workshops, or start your own networking group or book club? Will you go to lunch or coffee more often with your connections? How will this change your life and business?

LETTING OTHERS SEE OUR GREATNESS

One of my favorite soul sisters and best friends is Nung Rigor. She has become such an amazing friend, confidant and accountability partner. Nung and I met at a seminar, where we enjoyed a seven-day event, and made small talk. After that, we began meeting regularly for lunch and learned that we were both go-getter entrepreneurs, had children the same age and loved a lot of the same things. In short, we completely clicked. What I didn't know yet was the huge positive impact Nung would have on my career and life purpose.

At the time, I had just started life coaching as my full-time career. I had been doing it on the side for quite a few years in the past, and taking the seven-day course, along with my years of studying personal development and reading greats like Jim Rohn, Og Mandino and others, helped me realize it was my life's true purpose. Nung, who is in the field of life insurance, and I had started talking about building our businesses and supporting one another. One day we went to lunch and she asked me to speak at a large event with her. Although I had a degree in public speaking, as well as toastmasters and years of entertainment industry hosting and speaking experience, I had never thought of doing true inspirational speaking. At first, fear came up and I turned her down and made a bunch of excuses. Finally, however, after her encouragement and belief in me, I accepted.

The speaking engagement was my first for motivation and inspiration, but I had spoken many times in other arenas. I walked into the prestigious gardens country club feeling a bit nervous and realized that the talk was to be for a large group of young adults (ages 18-22), training to be camp counselors for the Los Angeles parks and recreation program. The problem was, they did not want to sit through a seminar on a pretty Saturday morning. They had been required and forced to be there. I looked out into a stream of yawns and cell phones being checked with heads on tables. As I was not experienced at this, I began writing my main points and notes on the giant white board that had been provided for me, so as not to forget my teachings. I began my talk with passion, enthusiasm and focus, and at first was very discouraged because my young audience was not amused.

I then decided that crying, giving up or walking out was not an option and raised my passion level up another notch. I began relating to the audience and building rapport through stories of my experience working with kids. As if a miracle had occurred for me, the young adults began sitting up, putting cell phones away and even taking notes. The rest of my one-hour talk was a success and I even had several attendees come up to me after, telling me that I had taught them something. I felt unstoppable, on fire and amazing. I knew at that moment in my life, I was meant to not only be a life coach, but a true inspirational speaker. If I could influence this group, I could do anything!

It went impressively well and was the start of my full true passion and purpose. Nung and I began doing workshops together at businesses and events and I started Willow Tree Circle, a connection group with empowering speakers and topics in Los Angeles and Orange County in Southern California every month. I began holding two events per month with much success, and ended up doing so for three years. I began speaking at large events, wrote a number one bestselling book, and created a life coaching certification program and ten week confidence course so I could begin passing on positive power to others.

Due to Nung's persuasiveness and her seeing in me what I had not seen in myself, I am now in my full positive power, doing what I love and touching lives. I truly learned to let others know the power and gifts you see in them as often as you can. They may not be able to see it themselves. Always be open-minded and optimistic. Be open to learning from others. If you feel that you know it all, opportunities and wisdom cannot enter. Finally, I learned that being around positive people has a huge impact on shifting your life to be even more amazing. Now, Nung and I take all of this positivity we learned and add it into our workshops and speaking engagements to touch others. That is true 10+ connecting and sisterhood.

10 TIPS FOR 10+ CONNECTING ON SOCIAL MEDIA FOR PERSONAL OR BUSINESS

1. Post a business post about the services or products you offer.

2. Post a personal post about what's going on in your personal life. For example, an exciting trip, some extraordinary news or something you've achieved.

3. Post a positive tip, affirmation or quote that you created or found.

4. Create a post that mixes personal with business. For example: I'm so happy I worked on my 10+ life coaching certification today. I have a lot of degrees that will add expertise to my coaching too.

5. Plug or promote someone else and tag him or her.

6. Post photos of you conducting business or enjoying personal activities. Example: speaking at an event, on a trip, meeting with a client or simply having fun.

7. Post any articles, media, radio shows or interviews you are featured in.

8. Post things you're celebrating that give you credibility and get attention.
Example: I'm so happy I'm halfway through being certified as a life coach.

Example: Wow so amazing! I'm speaking in front of 50 people for a business today.
Example: I'm honored and inspired to have my article featured on this blog. I just received an amazing testimonial about it.

9. Post testimonials about you or your business.

10. Last tip: Ask a question and get your audience involved.

Connect and collaborate with others. There is no competition: everyone is unique and different. If you were in a room with five others who did the same thing as you and had 200 potential clients, the right ones would magnetize to you because of who you are and what you bring.

10+ CONNECTING ACTIVITIES

Send out five messages today to five people who make you smile constantly and tell them why!

"You always make me smile because_____!"

Call an old friend, former teacher, mentor or colleague and tell them what they mean to you and how they have changed your life.

Go to a lounge, event, networking group or party and talk with three new people. Ask one to coffee or lunch. Email or message two new people per month to connect with.

List the people you'd like to connect with here.

_____
_____
_____
_____
_____
_____
_____
_____
_____
_____
_____
_____
_____

What collaborations would you like to plan with your connections?

10+ CONNECTION TIPS & AFFIRMATIONS

Friendships and relationships happen naturally. If there's force, trying, strain or worry involved, it's not flowing.

Remember to ask questions, learn about people you are talking with, smile and make eye contact. You might make a life-long friend.

Empathize with others; intuitively see them deep inside; realize they just need kindness and inspiration.

Who do you count as family? Family can be blood related as well as meaningful relationships with individuals that you love and love you.

Be a warm communicator; smile, ask questions, learn, be open and make others feel as if they've known you forever.

Relationships are the key to an empowered life.

Realize that each person, regardless of career or economic status, has something to teach us…something worthy to say.

It's simply not true that everyone has problems and nobody is truly happy. It REALLY is possible to be extremely happy in your life. Invest in your growth to greatness by spending time with positive people.

Talk to people everywhere; you never know whom you can help or what you will learn.

Be around the people you know that you'd miss if they weren't in your life. If you wouldn't miss them, think twice.

Aim daily to make others feel warm, welcome and happy with your kindness and enthusiasm.

Find the good in those you love. If you need to tell them something negative, find a kind and empowering way to say it.

Ask yourself if people are coming from love, friendship, needing attention or meaning well, to better empathize with them.

How many wonderful opportunities can I receive this month? How many amazing connections can I make with great people? How can I be my best self and radiate that out? These are powerful questions you can ask yourself, God and the universe.

Giving others the gift of generosity such as providing them with connections, advice, contacts, referrals and help is so much more wonderful and rewarding than being competitive.

Focus on love and repairing people's lives in need like those who are homeless, starving, abused pets or children. This is where some of the most productive, positive and peaceful energies can be directed.

Fill up your friends and family with gratitude, praise, love and kindness!

The fruit of your life are the friends, relationships, unique experiences and intimate moments and talks. Appreciate, cherish and remember them, for they are what make life amazing.

Do you place yourself on a pedestal and think you are more important than others? Or do you smile, laugh, connect and talk with everyone, realizing that people are all special in their own unique ways?

You are whom you are around. Spend time doing things that empower you with exciting people. Decide whom you'd like to know and take steps toward that connection.

Enlighten others with your wonderful presence, encourage them with your words, excite them with your wow factor and ease their fears and doubts with your wisdom.

What unique hobbies, interests or talents do you have that most people do not know about you?

CHAPTER THREE

10+
CORE

Your core is who you truly are. It is your essence, your being, your personality. It is what is uniquely you!

To love yourself more and figure out your gifts, strengths and talents, follow these steps:

- Acknowledge all you are good at, experiences you've had and the knowledge you've acquired.
- Have appreciation of what you contribute currently to the world.
- Assess where you are going, where you want to be and especially who you want to become.
- Work on becoming your best self, connect confidently and accept feedback and help from others.

As a result of taking these steps, this leads to accelerated success and a flowing fulfilling life. It is so worth it!

TIPS FOR SELF-LOVE AND SELF-AWARENESS

1. Get to know YOU by taking the time to self-reflect, analyze and take inventory.

2. Find and know your life purpose; know what makes you energized and fulfilled.

3. Be happy.

4. Be in your full positive power.

5. Create your own power phrase.

6. Ask eight people you trust to give you feedback.

7. Laugh at yourself more.

8. Live by example; walk the walk and talk the talk.

9. Keep photos of you at your best.

10. Look into the mirror until you love yourself: state positive affirmations. Never leave the mirror without thinking a good thought.

11. See beauty in everything.

12. Meditate and pray in nature.

13. Spend time in your garden, create art and sing.

14. Give hugs.

15. Celebrate successes.

16. Celebrate your uniqueness; no one has exactly what you have.

17. It's not about how much you have or have won, but how much you have given and loved.

18. Have someone to share with: accountability partner, mastermind group, etc. Announce your dreams and desires.

19. Don't be a part of the pity, grumbling or gossip party.

20. Don't compare yourself to others.

21. Surround yourself with positivity. Radiate happiness.

22. Not enough self-care leads to irritability, neediness, tiredness, overwork and self-pity. Take your time.

23. Continuously remember your true heart center, which is LOVE.

24. Ask yourself if your "shoulds" in life are facts or beliefs.

25. Live effervescently! Act vivacious and enthusiastic.

26. Continue growing, reading, learning and communicating. By doing this, you will always get better!

REFLECTION

What qualities about you can you OWN and let out more? Think of three things that you love about you, two that are unique about you, and one that you can celebrate about you. Put them all together and decide to radiate these qualities all month long. Journal how your life shifts!

You're perfect and on your way to even more 10+ dreams.

CONFIDENTLY FOLLOWING THE PATH OF YOUR HEART TO YOUR PASSIONS

Many people need help figuring out their passions, purpose and what makes them enthusiastic and excited about life. Figuring out and discovering your purpose and passions will make everything easier and clearer. Decisions will come naturally and opportunities will flow to you. You will become more fulfilled. It will reduce baggage and negativity, give enlightenment and clarity, improve relationships, extremely improve confidence, help you to make a difference, enable you to lead by example, find new careers, projects, hobbies and more. This is the most confident, intriguing, exciting and extraordinary way to live! Here is an exercise along with some questions that will help you to find your purpose and know yourself even better.

1. List the things you absolutely were thrilled to do as a child and teen (ages 3-17).

_____

_____

_____

_____

_____

_____

_____

2. Now, think back to the last six months and list the things you did that you were passionate and excited about.

_____
_____
_____
_____
_____
_____

3. Find the following items that will be symbols of yourself, your life and your passions, such as a photo, magazine clipping, an object or an item that represents the following:

   A. How you see yourself and your brand
   B. Prosperity and wealth
   C. Success, fulfillment and passion

   We learn the best through symbols. The words and symbols you use can have a profound effect on your well-being, success and overall mood.

   - What word/adjective describes each item?
   - What emotion does this make you feel?
   - What desire, dream or passion does it ignite?
   - What belief comes up when you discuss this?

Answer these here:

_____
_____
_____
_____
_____
_____
_____

10+ **CORE** | Living the 10+ Life   57

4. Now you should have several lists of words and descriptions. Take all of the lists and circle the words that "pop" or stand out to you. Now, narrow it down to the top 8 words or things that stand out.

___

5. Take these 8 words or descriptions and spend some time writing a paragraph on what each word means to you and your life. Take some time to realize how this fits into your purpose and passions.

___

6. Now, ask three of the closest people to you for feedback, where they can help you see your gifts, strengths and passions based on their knowledge of you and on what you found.

___

7. Finally, the most important strategy and piece of wisdom I have to offer is to confidently EXPECT. Expect means to decide with certainty that something is of your essence. It is a crucial ingredient!
EXPECT to succeed.
EXPECT to be happy.
EXPECT to have amazing friendships, love in your life, confidence and abilities.
EXPECT the best.
EXPECT that others see you just as the person who loves you most also sees you!

Train your brain to expect positivity. So many of us in our daily lives have gotten used to expecting the worst. We think things are going great but don't expect it to last for long. We need to realize that this is just learned behavior that can be unlearned. It stems from the past. Maybe we received a job offer and they changed their mind. A friend might have thrown an outdoor party for us and it rained. A great love relationship may have fizzled out. Yes, these experiences are difficult, but they do not have to shape the way we think today. We can use them as our life wisdom to fuel us forward toward bigger and better experiences and joys. If we can get our mind used to looking to the positive and expecting greatness for ourselves, we can put that energy out there which will attract the good.

8. Start this week by making a list of what good you expect to come. You will start to notice that your mind will begin taking more action toward opportunities. You will start attracting positive people. The more you receive, the stronger your confidence will become. The better your confidence and full positive power, the more exhilarating and amazing your life will become.

What good do you expect to come?

_____

_____

_____

_____

_____

_____

INTEGRITY IS ESSENTIAL

Having powerful, positive integrity, influence and reputation will naturally lead to huge success, fulfillment and joy.

Rate yourself on integrity, influence and reputation, in list below.

1. Walk the walk and talk the talk of whom you truly are.

2. Treat others with respect and kindness.

3. Always answer calls, emails and promises.

4. Go the extra mile when working, doing a project or helping someone.

5. Collaborate and connect instead of compete.

6. Give advice and help others authentically.

7. Continuously work on yourself, improving, growing and learning.

8. Smile often and sincerely compliment others.

9. Live by example.

10. Give back.

10+ CORE TIPS & AFFIRMATIONS

Perfect is peeling away the layers to get to the true you, embracing your own uniqueness, radiating who you truly are deep inside, feeling happy and fulfilled, creating your dreams and touching others' lives. You are already perfect and on your way to it even more.

Think about what makes you feel 100% you. Take those things and incorporate that into all that you do.

Beauty in a man or a woman is to be your complete true self and express yourself freely.

Be comfortable saying aloud the things you love about you! You are with yourself all day, so it is crucial to love yourself! Practice.

Discover your gifts; be open to them being revealed to you and giving yourself credit and power.

Your true heart's center is full of your true self, love, openness and positivity. Release what's covering it up and you will radiate from the inside out.

If you've experienced a loss of any kind, shift in your life, extra enlightenment lately or even a career change, you're due for a retreat! Take a trip, go to a spa, sit under a tree and write or even plan a camping outing.

You are meant to be Epic and Invincible in your own special way.

Be who you were born to be! Dare to plan out some adventures and excitement this year such as a vacation, concert, play, seminar, weekend road trip and more! Make at least one fun plan per month! Live for what makes you smile, feel passion, excited and enthusiastic!

A study just reported that the top regrets of those dying include not having lived their dreams, feeling fulfilled or living for other's expectations. Check yourself! What can you do starting now to begin living fulfilled, in your purpose, following your true heart?

Today, try to replace each complaint with gratitude. Let out your true self, embrace your uniqueness and let it shine out! Your brand consists of the aspects that attract others to you.

EMBRACE life with eagerness! Create your own opportunities and jump into them, ask for what you want and take action!

Dare to ask. Create your own spectacular opportunities and jump into them. Dream big and take action right away. Don't worry about failing. Simply let life flow and embrace the learning. Avoid competition because we are all unique and have gifts to offer the world.

Have the NERVE to be you; have the spunk, courage, bravery, boldness and heart. Have the ability to face "danger" without showing fear...

How do you accomplish this?

1. Work on who you, know yourself and what you truly want.
2. Visualize before each interaction and event... you being YOU.

Choose some interactions this week where you really let out the true you whether you were silly, dorky or awkward. Who cares, just be you!

10+ Tips for Being Social

S — Sharing who you truly are

O — Opening your heart

C — Caring

I — Involved

A — Accepting

L — Love people

CHAPTER FOUR

10+
COURAGE

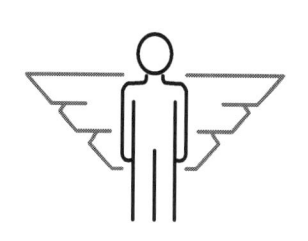

Focus on the goal of making space for greatness in your life at all times for growth, success, self-care, new people to enter and fulfillment.

These are steps and tools needed to get to where you are creating space and are ready for new opportunities and success to flow in.

1. SORT & SELECT

Sort through your life: what is working and what is not?

- Draw a stick figure and make a big circle around it with sections. This represents how much "space" you have. If your life is taken up with tasks and actions, you don't have any room for new adventures and opportunities to flow in.

- Next, take each space and write in your ideal life with dreams, goals and visions added in.

- Now, make another stick figure with sections and write in what you're doing overall in your life.

- What's taking up your energy? Label it positive, in between or negative to represent how it affects attaining the goals and dreams you noted on the first stick figure.

- Finally, how can you eliminate or cut back on the negative to make space?

2. PRACTICING POSITIVITY MAKES PERFECT

How will you practice positivity in the following areas?

- Your communication
- Your actions
- Your associations
- Your day-to-day life balance

_____
_____
_____
_____
_____

3. SOAR HIGH IN THE SKY

Awareness, appreciation, acknowledgement and attitude yield altitude, aka how high you will soar! Make sure you are self-aware, appreciate yourself and acknowledge your gifts.

How high will you soar?

_____
_____
_____
_____
_____

4. CREATE CONSCIOUSLY

Get curious about your life. What can be changed, shifted or improved? Where can you make space and then create your own opportunities and jump into them?

_____
_____
_____
_____
_____

5. EXECUTE ENTHUSIASTICALLY & ENERGETICALLY

Be excited about your life and the spaces you're creating. Sometimes people feel uncomfortable with the uncertainty. However, when we embrace the uncertainty we create more space.

What are you excited or uncertain about?

_____
_____
_____
_____
_____

6. CLEAN HOUSE

Sort out the clutter and negativity and select the creative and positivity so that you can start to sculpt the life you want by design.

What clutter will you eliminate?

_____
_____
_____
_____
_____

You have to be aware of yourself. You are the strong foundation. If you aren't completely aware and conscious of your choices, actions and abilities, you won't be able to have as many opportunities, events, adventures, people or positive power flow in.

POSITIVE POSSIBILITIES EXERCISE

This powerful exercise helps you to make fears, doubts and uncertainties disappear by magnifying all of the positive possibilities and shifting your brain into faith, confidence and courage.

1. List a fear, doubt or uncertainty related to life or business.

_____
_____
_____
_____
_____

2. What are you afraid of? List your fears.

_____
_____
_____
_____
_____

3. What are the positive possibilities? Try to list at least 50 positive possibilities.

4. List five reasons you deserve this.

_____

_____

_____

5. List five actions or changes to ensure you will get there.

_____

_____

_____

6. Are there any leftover fears or doubts?

_____

_____

_____

7. How can these be solved?

_____

_____

_____

8. Discuss plans.

_____

_____

_____

10+ COURAGE ACTIVITIES

List three amazing qualities you have that you bring to your business or life.

_____

_____

_____

How do you currently apply each quality right now? List at least two ways you use these for each quality.

_____

_____

_____

What are two ways you can and need to apply these qualities to enhance and improve you and your business today?

_____

_____

_____

What are your plans to start this?

_____

_____

_____

14 WAYS TO FLOW THROUGH FEAR

14 tips to help you powerfully flow through fear and create courage.

1. Rate the people in your life and the tasks you are involved in (0-100%). Only do the things and see the people that are 90-100% on your list, as this adds joy, direction and focus. Since you are passionate and excited by all you're doing and whom you're with, it is very difficult for real fear to enter. You're on fire, focused and fueled.

2. Know what you truly want in life, why you want it, who will help you and what it will look and feel like when you get it. Knowing this for each goal will fuel and make you stronger than any fears that pop up. Find doubts and objections that are there and create solutions to fix them.

3. Turn fear into childlike curiosity, fun and wonder.

4. Immerse yourself into positive, energized focus with each task, goal and activity. Be so into it and so in the now that you don't have time for fear.

5. Be immersed and absorbed in what you do. Go with the flow acting focused and free. Be open-minded, optimistic and appreciate the wonders of the world.

6. Have awareness of what you're afraid of. Where is it coming from? Next, shift it to the positive opposite. Switch it to gratitude, excitement and faith. For example, if you are scared of what

clients are thinking, you're mixing worry with pessimism; shift it. Instead of mixing worry with pessimism, perhaps we shift it to hope and optimism, seeing it as an opportunity to make a positive impression.

7. Get feedback throughout. Ask for help from those you trust for feedback on how you're doing and how you can be better.

8. Be persistent, it pays off. Have faith that it will work out as it is meant to.

9. Have low self-centeredness by practicing connection, collaboration and giving.

10. Visualize your outcome. See, hear and experience it.

11. Follow your heart, inner scale and intuition.

12. Expand your horizons and push yourself to go bold. Train your mind that you are courageous.

13. Think of ways you conquered fears in the past. Think of one now...how did you feel?

14. Remember past memories of you being bold, brave and fearless.

LET GO OF PAIN

This exercise releases pain and low energy emotions to heal and make room for confidence and success.

1. Draw a picture of yourself when you were born. This should show you free and filled with love and joy.

2. Now circle one layer around you for each significant hurt, bad experience or negative emotion that has happened to you that you feel you have held on to.

3. Study it realizing that these walls and layers can be healed, let go, removed and shifted. By holding onto them you are punishing yourself.

4. Write a list of everyone you're angry, bitter, upset and disgusted with.

5. Keep this list with you for one day and let yourself be bitter, angry, sad, upset, and confused. This allows these walls and layers to rise to the surface, therefore making it easier to remove them.

6. After the day, look at your list and decide to label each one as forgiveness, not for the behavior, but for yourself. Each one has a label. For example, he did this to me because he's sick in the mind or that teacher said that because she had a hard childhood.

7. Next, do a ceremony where you let all of this go to be free, move on and heal. Take your paper and rip it up and set it on fire over a sink or trash can and watch it go away. This symbolizes that you're letting go and moving forward.

Remember this when you feel low, irritated, stressed or hopeless; it's just a reminder of who you are NOT. Step out and look within to your true powerful self that is strong and confident.

Look into the mirror by first taking anything negative that comes up. Write it down and drown it in a bowl of water. Then, look and find five things you love.

Smile and say them out loud finishing with, "I LOVE MYSELF!"

WAYS TO PUSH FORWARD PAST FEAR, DOUBT AND MEDIOCRITY… FOCUS ON WHAT YOU TRULY WANT

1. Be the opposite of mediocre. Instead of average, unexciting and forgettable, be enthusiastic, confident and memorable. Stand out from the crowd and go the extra mile. Connect, give and do more than you're paid for.

2. Ask yourself regularly how you're doing. Check in. When making decisions or evaluating parts of your life, ask yourself the following:
   - Where, like a car, do you feel fueled? Or, do you feel flattened like a flat tire? When something naturally fuels you, it feels like a propelling energy.
   - What areas do you feel in the flow, in a funk or forced?
   - Where do you feel fantastic or feel like a failure?
   - Where do you feel like you're doing something with finesse or feel like a fraud?

Answer these here:
_____
_____
_____

3. All that you do and who you are with is a mirror for how high your confidence is.

4. Focus in on what the fear really is and then list the positive possibilities that can negate those fears from coming to fruition.

List the fears here:

_____

_____

_____

List the positive possibilities here:

_____

_____

_____

Don't let this happen to you:

- One day I'll be living that way, one day I'll be a famous _____, one day I'll have the right friends, one day I'll leave this negative person or place.

Instead:

- Decide right now that you'll take a BOLD step toward the way you want, deserve and truly can live your life. Read stories of those who triumphed over tragedy, ask for help, keep moving forward, own what you're doing and others will too.
- Think of the times you flowed through fear, did it anyway and came out fantastic! This will train your mind that you can do it again and again. Bigger, better, brighter and bolder!

What one thing are you going to boldly step forward toward today?

_____

_____

_____

BE YOU

Have the NERVE to be you; have the spunk, courage, bravery, boldness, heart and the ability to face "danger" without showing fear.

1. Work on who you are by knowing yourself and what you truly want.

2. Visualize before each interaction and event.

3. Choose some interactions this week where you really let out the true you.

4. Move forward fearlessly toward your passions. Take action now.

What actions will you take to follow your passions?

_____
_____
_____
_____
_____
_____
_____
_____
_____
_____
_____
_____

BENEFITS OF HIRING A LIFE COACH

To think we can always see ourselves clearly or know how others see us can be delusional. Life coaching can help with this. It can be a way to ask for help and how to grow, learn, achieve more and soar.

Life coaching can absolutely help you to love your life, feel fulfilled and live an extraordinary life. Six to twelve months of coaching can shape, change and improve your life in amazing ways. It can help you tap into who you truly are and get you to your highest potential.

It's never too late to achieve, grow and become! You can begin to bloom today!

In what areas would you like to feel extraordinary?

_____

_____

_____

_____

_____

_____

_____

_____

_____

_____

_____

_____

_____

10+ COURAGE TIPS & AFFIRMATIONS

When things change, get cancelled or don't work out, realize that you now have space for something or someone greater to come into your life. Don't be disappointed. Be excited and trust!

Fear is most often created and imagined; it's anticipating the worst scenario. Instead, realize that you CAN do it by visualizing success and anticipating amazing things.

Remove sections of doubt from your being and replace them with KNOWING and CERTAINTY. You were born to soar!

Which is easier: Staying in anger, guilt, fear, pain and sorrow or moving forward in love, compassion, gratitude and joy?

Let music elevate your mood, state and being.

What's easier: Being stuck in depression, anger and frustration or finding the good around you and moving forward? Instead of fretting over what you could have, should have and would have, always do the best you can so you'll feel at peace.

Make the space in your life for your true desires to enter. Go for it!

Opportunities of positivity, inspiration and excitement will flow to you because you are open to them and READY!

Take your time in your life journey as rushing implies fear of failure. Live with ease, grace and knowing. Feel your highest self and make decisions that way. Flow with life!

Remind yourself that all you've gone through has given you wisdom and courage, made you non-judgmental and given you the tools to help others.

Leave behind the thoughts that you don't compare, you're not good enough or don't have enough to say. Remember that deep inside, you have your full power that wants to come out!

Throw away thoughts that you cannot do something. Instead, ask for help, take action, research how and believe!

What beliefs or patterns are holding you back? When you think or say something negative, ask yourself if it is a fact. Many times it is just a belief that you have the power to shift and change into something empowering.

Are you living like a victim of circumstances? Instead, choose to find solutions by letting go and starting now. Ask for help, search, move forward and make positive changes. Live like a fan with three speeds. You're in control whether you take action at a light speed, move at a medium motion or move forward fearlessly with passion that propels you to your goals at high speed.

You decide. Dare to pray for, expect and accept huge miracles in your life such as money marvels, health wonders, happiness, passion and joy!

Redefine your vulnerability as openness to new people, ideas and opportunities. This turns into curiosity and power.

If you feel it in your heart, soul and you want it but you are scared, do it anyway.

Being open-minded means being powerful, kind and wise. You can truly learn from everyone you encounter. Perhaps it's learning how you don't want to be, but more often you can gain insight from someone you run into at a random store, at your business, at a networking event. Sometimes people believe if they are an important CEO, they cannot talk to the janitor or vice versa. If you have no ego controlling the real you, you can appreciate and learn from everybody.

Even when life has tribulations or problems, focus on the gifts that come out of them during and after.

Next time a big problem or hardship appears, do not label it as such. Look for the gifts right away but still feel the sting of it. Begin looking for positive solutions. By taking action, that problem or hardship will become a blessing, gift and growth opportunity. It will amaze you.

Heal from guilt about your past. Forgive yourself and take action to be better, do better and use past mistakes to be wiser. It does no good to keep punishing your body and mind. Instead, use it as fuel to be great! Sometimes you need to learn who you don't want to be so that you can be your best self.

Just ask! You might get 50 no's, ignores or maybes, but those few yeses are what change your life.

CHAPTER FIVE

10+
CREATIVE EXPRESSION

To truly know you are making the right, passionate, in tune and aligned choices to create your most wonderful life, make sure you are clear on your intentions for everything you do, your communication, your relationships and your life's purpose. Lead yourself, focus, be clear, motivate and inspire yourself to move forward with purpose, intention, passion and action. Live by example.

Simplify your life by doing everything aligned with your purpose. You know you love what you do when you eagerly wake up and jump into action, starting work right away. With this mindset it's not really work, but it's fun, passion and purpose! Yes, it's possible.

Free yourself from thinking you HAVE to meet other's expectations or please everyone. Live according to your purpose, true self and what makes you feel joy and harmony. Great things come to those who have purpose, intention, positive action and communication with people around them.

When you meet in a group of positive people with amazing energetic goals, the energy increases, creating a powerful positive vibration and frequency that yields sensational successes, further resulting in life changing happiness.

With whatever you do in life as your passion and purpose, make sure you're an expert. Walk the walk and talk the talk and be living it by getting better and growing daily. A sense of fulfillment is when every part of you is in harmony with passion and enthusiasm. Develop a sense of strong certainty and knowing that your life will soon soar even more positively.

0-100% EXERCISE

This is a powerful exercise to build confidence by only spending time with people and taking actions that are 100% in your heart and soul. There are exceptions with paying taxes, doing laundry and things you must do that none of us seem to enjoy. However, this method truly helps with saying "no more" and tuning into what you really want, which is a huge way to exude confidence.

1. Make three columns on a sheet of paper.

2. In column one, spend about 15 minutes listing the standout projects, achievements, exciting memories and things about you that stand out from when you were a baby to now.

3. In column two, list what you are currently doing with your time and energy.

4. In column three, list your dreams, goals and visions.

5. Next, go back and rate each item in all three columns from 0% to 100%. Zero being that you despise it, and 100% being that you're on fire, in love and passionate about it.

6. Then, go back and circle items only from 90-100% with the goal being that you focus on things in your life that you love.

7. Finally, go forward with goal setting.

Consider the emotions of feeling alive, spirited, exuberant and energetic. Be with who makes you exuberant, do what makes you flourish, go where you are most yourself, create what makes you experience passion, love who makes you energetic and say what makes you feel alive.

Remember that competition is a low energy and involves fear, lack and jealousy. Exude love!

GOALS

PROJECTS & ACHIEVEMENTS

TIME & ENERGY NOW

DREAMS, GOALS & VISIONS

PRACTICE THE FOUR P'S

POWERFUL

POSITIVE

PURPOSEFUL

PRESSURE

Work on yourself, spend time with great people, eliminate negative influences and habits, move forward fearlessly and take TRUE action toward what you want!

What do you intensely dream of doing one day?

_____

_____

What could you do to get the ball rolling?

_____

_____

What is holding you back, who do you need to ask for help?

_____

_____

What small steps of action could get you started?

_____

_____

A LEADER

L — Loves people
E — Energy is contagious
A — Allows opportunities to enter
D — Dreams big
E — Enthusiastic
R — Radiates success, authenticity, confidence and power

What qualities of a leader do you have?

_____
_____
_____
_____
_____
_____

What can you do to develop some of the other necessary qualities that a leader possesses?

_____
_____
_____
_____
_____
_____

When hearing your own inner self talk, ask yourself, is this a fact or am I creating my own drama, beliefs and rules? Instead, tell yourself what you truly want. Shoot for your dreams, goals, passions, heart's true purpose and what you love. Focus on what thrills you, fulfills you, embraces your inner child, makes you anticipate amazing things every day and creates an amazing life.

Following your passion makes life easier, more fulfilling and enables you to be a living example. For some people in today's times, a new business or a side business can lead to greater income, freedom and stability. For others, moving up or growing in their current career is inspirational. Ultimately, finding your deep dreams, passions and purpose is the key to getting every area of your life to a 10+.

6 TIPS AND TOOLS TO FUEL YOU

1 Make space for greatness by evaluating where you are now, how that is working for you and where you would love to be next year. Say "no" to or get rid of several things.

_____

_____

_____

_____

2 Create three BIG goals you will achieve no matter what, and add the steps needed to achieve them.

_____

_____

_____

_____

3 Make a list of the people in your life now. Analyze whom you want to spend more and less time with. Additionally, figure out whom you want to add in.

_____

_____

_____

4. Make a list of all of your best qualities inside and out. Place stars next to the attributes and qualities you will embrace, emphasize and let shine even more. Add in new items where you will improve and grow. Maybe you will become a better writer or begin wearing brighter colors more often.

___

5. Plan your retreats and travels for the year ahead. This will motivate and inspire you to look forward to adventures and fuel you to manifest the money and means to do so.

___

6. Decide who will be your coach or mentor. We all need one to think outside of our own brainpower. Also, create a mastermind group or find an accountability partner to talk with often to soar toward success.

___

10+ CREATIVE EXPRESSION TIPS & AFFIRMATIONS

Your life purpose will guide you in how you make all your decisions, what to do, what to say and who to spend time with.

Be an expert. Live by example. Walk the walk and talk the talk!

A sense of fulfillment is when every part of you is in harmony with passion, purpose and enthusiasm.

Be clear on your intentions for everything you do, your communication, your relationships and your life's purpose.

Do crazy wonderful things that create memories! Dance in the bathroom with your kids, jump up and sing at concerts, surprise someone with a day trip somewhere exciting and more.

WOW = Watch Out World!

Make shopping like a dream board; each time you purchase a dress, outfit or pair of hot shoes, visualize yourself doing something spectacular wearing it, succeeding and celebrating, and you will create and feel that again when you wear it.

POWER AFFIRMATION

This week thank you God for positive and extraordinary people and huge opportunities coming into my life that I accept with grace, ease and balance!

POWER MANTRA

Feel big opportunities coming in this month. It's a feeling of flowing, letting go, letting God, a buzz, an excitement, a knowing, a fun anticipation of what's to come.

You know how children laugh, scream, shout and dance anytime, anywhere and whenever they want? This is why adults go to sporting events and ride roller coasters. Dare to do this whenever you feel like it. Don't limit yourself, but embrace and celebrate your inner child.

HOW TO LIVE WITH INTEGRITY

Walk your walk. Talk your talk. Keep your promises. Call and explain if you have to cancel, but try not to. Do your absolute best. Practice going the extra mile. Smile; be real, genuine and authentic. Show appreciation, gratitude and love of life and yourself. You will certainly go far in life if you live these simple ways that most choose not to. Start today. This builds and grows your character and creates a shining reputation.

CHAPTER SIX

10+
CONSCIOUSNESS

GOING WITH THE FLOW AS AN ENTREPRENEUR AND A MOTHER

I love being a woman. It is so fabulous being able to be a mom, wife, friend, career woman, entrepreneur and more, all with the essence of femininity. I think it is an empowering, fun and exciting life. Your perspective is the key to get to the place where you feel this way too. I like to use the acronym and word, FLOW, as a regular reminder that flowing with life is the ideal way to live and balance all of the roles we are involved in.

The **F** stands for **FOCUSED**. It is important to live a focused life, concentrating on what we want and not on what it is we do not want or need. We can stay focused on what is important, meaningful, our goals, our family, our daily lives and especially self-care such as exercise, eating right, dressing nice and looking our best. By flowing through life with focus, we can achieve more, but do not need to obsess about every little thing. If we make a mistake or miss a workout, we forgive ourselves and keep moving forward.

The **L** stands for **LOVE** and **LET GO**. It is amazing to live from your heart with love, kindness, inspiration for others and yourself and grace. Let yourself live this way and feel the uplifting energy it brings you. At the same time, learn to let go. Do not get too attached to how you think things should be, how others are supposed to act or what was not said. See the good.

The **O** stands for **OPTIMISTIC**. Living with optimism is seeing the light versus the dark in each person, situation and place. How can you contribute your smile, enthusiasm and positivity daily? Be open to seeing the good in others. It can be challenging at times, but it is so worth it.

The W stands for the WONDERS of the WORLD. Appreciate nature, beauty and yourself. See the small things in life such as your child's laugh, that hug from your best friend, the birds singing on your roof and the tall trees around your neighborhood as the miracles that they are.

Remembering this will help you to stay in the flow of life with ease and joy. It will allow you to be a better mother or father, friend, businesswoman or businessman and overall person. Additionally, it makes you feel uplifted daily. Go ahead and try it!

HOW TO MAKE A DIFFERENCE

1. Volunteer.

2. Smile genuinely.

3. Contribute creatively with art, music, blogs, books, poetry, teachings and more.

4. Help others.

5. Communicate positively.

6. Radiate out love and peace from your heart and being.

7. Grow daily, become your best self via study, self-inventory and experiences.

8. Check your beliefs. Are they facts? Do they make you feel high or low vibrations? How are they working for you?

9. Focus on miracles, faith and joy as much as you can.

10. Embrace nature, God and the universe.

TIPS AND TOOLS TO SHIFT STRESS INTO SERENITY AND SUCCESS

As we experience our daily lives, the days can be filled with phone calls, work and driving all over the place. It can get a bit crazy and demanding, making us think we have to be super heroes. Many of us aspire to be perfect. When we mess up or do not follow through, we often feel bad about ourselves, which puts us in a negative and disempowered state of mind.

It is important to forgive ourselves and do the best that we can. Rewarding ourselves and celebrating our successes helps us to stay motivated. Remember that a bad mood is just a low energy state and we have the power to shift out of it.

Here are some ways we can change the energy from negative to positive:

1. Give! Hug your spouse, significant others, friends or kids. Blow kisses more often. Do volunteer work, go help out a friend, smile at a child or call a family member. Giving helps you forget your troubles and feels great.

2. Go do something fun and exciting that you loved to do as a child either alone, on a date or with your own kids. Build a sand castle, hula-hoop, eat a peanut butter and jelly sandwich or take a day trip to Disneyland. Embrace your inner child and remember who you truly are.

3. Read an uplifting and inspirational book. Talk to an encouraging person, choose a mentor to regularly learn from and watch a motivating or funny DVD. Smile more. Shout in the car empowering words such as "I am powerful!"

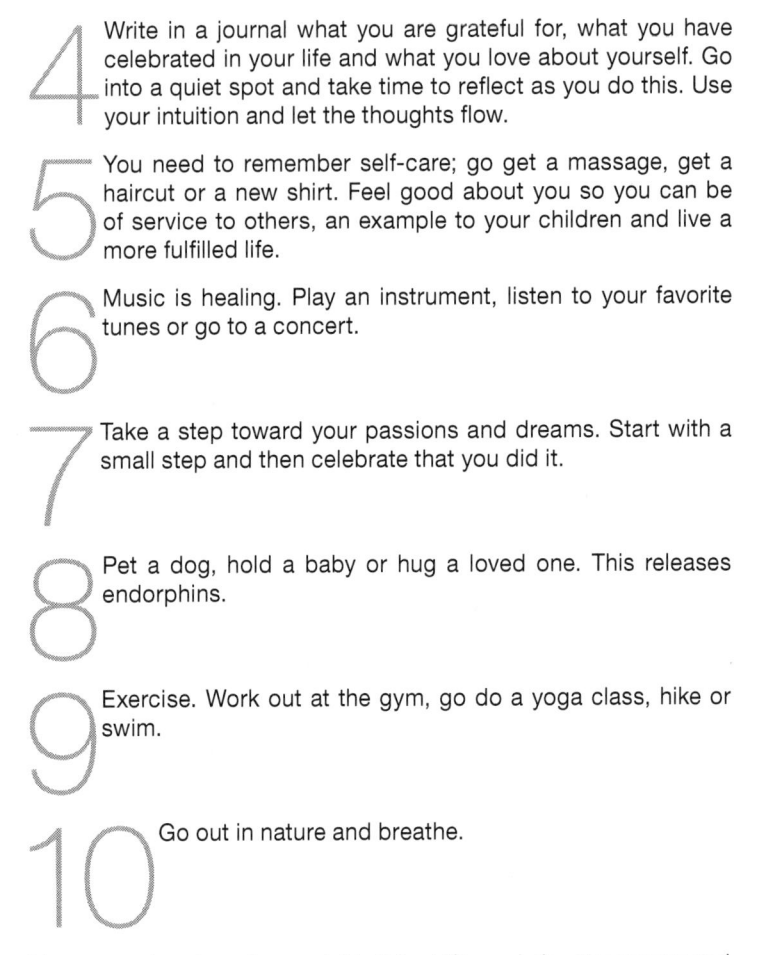

4. Write in a journal what you are grateful for, what you have celebrated in your life and what you love about yourself. Go into a quiet spot and take time to reflect as you do this. Use your intuition and let the thoughts flow.

5. You need to remember self-care; go get a massage, get a haircut or a new shirt. Feel good about you so you can be of service to others, an example to your children and live a more fulfilled life.

6. Music is healing. Play an instrument, listen to your favorite tunes or go to a concert.

7. Take a step toward your passions and dreams. Start with a small step and then celebrate that you did it.

8. Pet a dog, hold a baby or hug a loved one. This releases endorphins.

9. Exercise. Work out at the gym, go do a yoga class, hike or swim.

10. Go out in nature and breathe.

Now, go out and see how quickly this shifts and elevates your mood and state. Try these often to uplift your life and experience a lot more joy so that you can meet your goals and resolutions and experience exciting adventures.

What will you regularly do to get rid of stress?

Appreciate the small things, the fine details, each comment you make, your friends and your surroundings. Add more fun and play to your life and receive more calmness, peace and overall abundance and success. Spend time making quality memories doing things you love in your heart and soul. See yourself where you want to be but enjoy where you are now too.

Pour your heart into what you are passionate about! Be aware of what you are doing and see the beauty in it. Find the uniqueness in each situation and follow your heart to where you want to go, those you want to be with and what you want to do.

MAKING POWERFUL TRANSFORMATIONS

Whenever it feels like your time is the time to begin transforming your life. What will change for the better? Instead of just making resolutions like you are supposed to be doing, why not DECIDE? Decide that you will have your most amazing year yet. Make the decision to boost your confidence and self-esteem by working on you. Start now by eliminating anything negative including bad habits, hanging around the wrong people or spending time on what drains you. Start now by adding positivity, meeting new great connections and taking steps toward your passions. Some ideas to start this year are join a networking group, attend positive seminars or make plans with a friend one day per week to talk, have lunch and laugh. Make a list of what you enjoyed doing when you were younger and start doing those things again. This helps remind your brain that you have passion and enthusiasm for life, and often helps you find your new hobby, career or project. Finally, spend time on things that fuel you. You will know they are your passions because you feel elevated when involved with these things. This will increase your confidence because you are proving to yourself that you care about you.

A powerful way to ensure success is to check in with your thoughts at least three times per day with curiosity and awareness. Consider the following questions: *Who am I with? What am I doing? How am I communicating and behaving? Which direction is my life going? Am I living my passions?* Get into this positive and productive habit, making sure to regularly adjust, alter and adapt your life by design. Decide that this will be your most adventurous, exciting and amazing year yet. Go buy a planner and map it out. Plan your trips, outings, career moves, workshops and events. This daily reminder will allow you to see the good and take steps each day toward passion, confidence, peace and happiness. Flow with life, exude authenticity, kindness and integrity. Appreciate each moment and celebrate life to the fullest. You deserve it.

What is your vision for transforming your life?

HOW TO HAVE A SPECTACULAR LIFE

Do you want to have the kind of life that is excitingly appealing, glamorous and filled with adventure; a life where you reveal the real you, your truest self, living on purpose with passion? You truly can!

Here are some tips and tools for living the life of a sexy, spectacular star. You deserve it.

1. Plan something exciting at least three times per month; this can be a trip, an event, dinner with friends, going to a fabulous art museum, horseback riding and more.

2. Schedule vacations.

3. Hang around exciting people; decide whom you'd like to know and take steps toward that. This is living with intention.

4. Follow your heart and do something you're passionate about daily.

5. Make a list of things you dislike doing but need to do and make them fun, creative or unique.

6. Turn on music and dance.

7. Dress up.

8. Reward yourself.

9. Watch, attend, read or listen to something meaningful; learn and grow.

10. Get bold and out of your comfort zone and try something new.

What three negative things can you remove from your life to make room for positive?

_____

_____

_____

_____

_____

Vacations are so significant: balance, de-stress, fun and adventure. Where are you going this year?

_____

_____

_____

_____

_____

You always have choices in life! Take the time to make positive decisions moving forward.

Never feel guilt for treating yourself well. Make time for spa days, walks on the beach and lunch with good friends. Do this regularly and you will succeed, be fulfilled and love yourself even more!

10+ CONSCIOUSNESS TIPS & AFFIRMATIONS

The Power of choice is so unique to humans.
Animals do not grasp this concept.
We have the opportunity to choose our life path.
Who are we hanging out with?
What are we doing?
Are we following our heart?

If you're messing up in life,
take charge of your power and choices.
Choose to get help, make new decisions,
change your life to how you truly deserve to live.

Create the life you want.
A sprinkle of positivity,
a handful of confidence,
a bowl of believing you can do it,
jars and jars of action
and a barrelful of amazing people in your life.

Instead of complaining, create.
Instead of grumbling, have gratitude.
Instead of fear, have faith.
Instead of lack, have love.
Instead of envy, have enthusiasm.
Instead of patience, have intrigue.

Look at your life and fall in love with it!

Focusing on the beauty will bring in miracles.

The key is feeling that your life is amazing now and that everything else coming in is a huge bonus. This is *Living the 10+ Life*.

Trust your intuition. Let it lead you to the flourishing people, choices and outcomes.

Treat days off like your vacation. Fall in love with your city; embrace the sights, museums, events and nature of where you live.

What are three words that describe what you need for joy in each area of your life?

Example: Passion, Enthusiasm and Inspiration

What words do you use more: passionate, delightful, amazing, extraordinary, awesome, annoying, frustrating, stressed or angry? The words you choose to use shape your life.

Opportunities pop up when you expect them, and have faith that they will.

When negative or self-defeating thoughts arise, pretend your mind is an Etch A Sketch and just shake and clear away quickly and easily until clear.

Instead of talking bad about others or judging, find the good in them by really empathizing with where they're coming from. Open your mind to people teaching you something this week. Ask interesting questions. Surprise them.

CHAPTER SEVEN

10+
COMMUNICATION, CHOICES & CREATIONS

10 STEPS TO DAILY MAGNIFICENT MOMENTS

The hustle and bustle of life often leads to us becoming robotic, unaware and numb to our emotions. We get so used to rushing, climbing to achieve our next goal and wanting more, that we can forget what life can bring. How can we be in the moment, take action but also just let life flow? Focus on the moments, memories, miracles and meaning in life. This is what matters. This is what leads to joy, fulfillment, success and satisfaction. The key is practicing this.

Reference these 10 steps to having magnificent moments daily:

1. Meaning

Look for the meaning each day in all you do. What does your day look like? How can you make the moments of your day filled with meaning? Compliment a stranger, call a friend and say you appreciate them or go to a spectacular event.

2. Open-Minded

Look at everything with an open mind. Be open to opportunities, humor, laughter, possibilities, miracles, new connections, learning something new, beauty and smiles.

3. Mindfulness

Focus on each moment – body sensations, thoughts, feelings, vibes and energy. Accept the feelings and thoughts.

4. Enthusiasm

Intense, eager enjoyment, express yourself fully.

5. Be in the Now

Practice living, grounding, and meditation. Breathe, notice colors, inner child behaviors and activities.

6. Throw Away Thoughts

Train your mind to understand what isn't working for you.

7. Sculpt Your Life by Design

Check in by asking questions, setting goals, visualizing and being intentional.

8. Enhance Success

Utilize your resources with seminars, CDs, books, positive places, people and communication.

9. Believe You Can and You Will

Imagine the possibilities; then make them realities with action, faith, purpose and passion!

10. Free Your Mind of Beliefs That Hold You Back

Soar forward with redefined power thoughts and actions.

7 WAYS TO PRACTICE FEELING EXHILARATED!

1. Practice not concealing or downplaying your enthusiasm, excitement or joy. Instead, practice just letting it out!

2. Be with people who ELEVATE YOU! They should lift you up, put you in a cheerful mood, inspire, encourage and are kind to you; AND YOU TO THEM! This alone is life changing!

3. EXPECT! Expect means to decide with certainty that something is of your essence (a crucial ingredient).

   EXPECT to succeed, EXPECT to be happy, EXPECT to have amazing friendships, love in your life, confidence and abilities, EXPECT the best, EXPECT that others see you as the person who loves you most also sees you! Train your brain to EXPECT positivity. Make a list of the greatness you are going to start expecting right now!

_____

_____

_____

_____

_____

4. CHANGE your language, vocabulary and communication to empowering words, seeing the best in each situation. Practice and it starts to become natural, without even trying.

5. EMBRACE life with eagerness! Create your own opportunities and jump into them, ask for what you want and take action.

6. Step aside, look in and consider what else is needed to make our life whole. Are you fulfilled and all else is a bonus? If you are not there yet, what will it take to get there? If you were giving someone else advice on this, what would you say?

_____

_____

_____

_____

_____

_____

7. Growth, knowledge, connections and experiences equal power and effectiveness, moving forward and climbing to the top. Think back over your life from a child to now. What has made you feel exhilaration that you can start doing again? What new things can you try?

_____

_____

_____

_____

_____

_____

HOW TO BE IN EACH EXPERIENCE AND MOMENT

Show up, truly be there, embrace each moment and person, share insights, inspiration, tools and knowledge.

Try throwing out all of your complaints, negative opinions, aches, pains, worries and fears. Start with a clean slate. I give you permission to start today and this week and even all of the year and on flowing, free, fearless and fabulous!

In order to have success, it is important to exude confidence in all you do. You can do a self-evaluation and ask yourself these questions: *Am I doing what I love? Do I feel that I could be doing more? Am I making positive life decisions daily? What could I start doing today to be more confident?* These powerful questions will help you to realize whether you need to make a few changes in your life to be happier and feel great about you. Inspired ideas for your life can start your power flowing and will help you move forward and enjoy your life even more.

Are you conforming or fitting the stereotype of the type of person you are, career you are in or the way you live? Do you want to live like that, or is it time to shift, shape and sculpt your life by design?

It's time to think outside the box, push past your usual comfort levels and get to some enhanced success. Happiness really is the most important thing. Not what "they" might think, not what will bring you the most popularity, not what seems like the thing to do, but instead what makes you truly happy and fulfilled.

What can happen is the accumulation of negativity, clutter and not checking in with yourself, and soon you are living robotically and your life is full but not filled with what you ideally want. This is when feelings of bitterness and unhappiness creep in.

If you aren't completely aware and conscious of your choices, actions and abilities, you won't be able to have as many opportunities, events, adventures, people or positive power flowing in. Journal what shifts you will make to transform your life now.

DISAPPOINTED? HOW TO LOOK FOR THE GIFT OR OPPORTUNITY

1. Decide what opportunities would make your passion, purpose, project pursuit or profession soar, succeed or move forward in big ways. Make a list of two:

_____
_____
_____
_____
_____

2. Self Promotion: have 10-30 things you love about you as the foundation in your mind. Which four resonate with what you're doing here most? Next, for one week, write to or connect with three people each day to ask for advice, guidance or ideas on these, ask for opportunities and possibly even strategic partners. Make sure to add these qualities about yourself and get comfortable mentioning them on paper and in person.

_____
_____
_____
_____

3. Next, think of ways that you can create these opportunities on your own. Think bold and outside of the box. Take time to brainstorm a list of ideas all over your journal whether they are crazy, fun or wild. List some to start:

_____

_____

_____

_____

_____

4. Ask yourself, who else does what I want to do? How did they get there? Research this to gather even more ideas. Go to specific networking events to connect with people. Keep learning so you become the guru in your profession and can own what you do.

_____

_____

_____

_____

_____

5. Meet with an accountability partner at least once every week by phone or in person to review, gather ideas and receive feedback. List ideas of great people to partner with:

_____

_____

_____

_____

_____

6. Create plans of action. Prioritize all of the ideas. Which are the 100% ideas that feel exciting, amazing and powerful? Take the top idea and begin with that. Break it into small steps and create a schedule and time frame for moving forward.

_____

_____

_____

_____

_____

7. Make sure to take steps right away. Action will fuel you and show results.

8. As soon as you step into one of your self-created opportunities, celebrate and keep going!

9. Journal the results, connections, credibility and success. Own it!

10. Be ready when the bigger opportunities come as a result of this. Make sure to imagine, visualize and see the money flowing in.

4 IMPORTANT A's

1. Applaud – Celebrate your successes and your steps to greatness. How often do you applaud your own successes?

2. Acknowledgement – Have the courage, strength and nerve to truly be YOU. Do you feel that you are 100% yourself with everyone, everywhere?

3. Abilities – Know what it takes to have effectiveness, power, skills and belief in yourself. Are you aware of your abilities and endless possibilities?

4. Appreciation – Truly realize you can learn from everyone. Have genuine appreciation. NO HIERARCHY OR COMPETITION.

Challenge: go through the weekend beginning now not complaining. Catch yourself. Check if you are complaining or just explaining.

Change is a gift. It creates miracles! It can be anything involving growing, evolving, changing, creating or transformation.

Are you around high or low energy choices regularly?
Do you elevate others and yourself by a smile or a frown?

When making a decision, act as though you have an inner scale.
What weighs more, your intuitive no or your intuitive yes?
Tune in because you already know the answer!

When feeling negative, make yourself think of seven things that represent love and you'll feel much better.

List seven things that represent love below:

_____
_____
_____
_____
_____
_____
_____
_____
_____

Give compliments freely and remember to accept them deeply as well.

Have tenacity to keep moving forward, even when obstacles come.

Create a gratitude list; then go for your wildest dreams, knowing that even if you fall on your face, you always have what's on your gratitude list! List ten things you are grateful for, and why:

_____
_____
_____
_____
_____
_____
_____
_____
_____
_____
_____
_____

Would you go to your own business or use your own service? This way of thinking is a great way to rate your life.

Ask yourself: am I one of those people that return calls and emails quickly, say please and thank you, do what I say I'm going to do, walk the walk and talk the talk, help others without expecting something in return and give compliments freely? These are essentials to success and happiness.

The qualities of humility, integrity, kindness, compassion and tenacity are so-called rare traits. Commit to having these qualities and stand out in the world.

Are you one of these people? What can you improve upon?

_____

_____

_____

_____

_____

Try something new for 30 days. Start a PEOPLE journal and each day write whom you connected with, helped, complimented and hugged, who you made an impact on and who really touched your heart. See how your life changes! Start by listing today.

_____

_____

_____

_____

_____

Remember and visualize old achievements, positive occurrences, great memories and childhood fun. These are proof to yourself that you can feel, see, hear, do and experience these wonderful gifts again and go even further.

THINKING OUTSIDE THE BOX

Thinking outside the box is more than just a business cliché. It requires approaching problems in new and innovative ways. It compels us to conceptualize problems differently and understand your position in relation to any particular situation in a way you'd never thought of before. Ways to think outside the box:

1. Ask a child or several kids.

2. Draw! Use a pen, colored pencils or crayons.

3. Read and learn something new by taking a new class or attending a new seminar.

4. Review various magazines for ideas.

5. Search power words and items on the Internet with a journal.

6. Journal freestyle.

7. Change your location, space and routine.

Example: Writer, Toni Morrison, watched the sun come up in the morning before she would begin writing. She felt that this enabled her to access her creativity.

8. Brainstorm: Avoid limiting yourself when you're brainstorming. This is the time when all ideas are welcome, no matter how silly or unworkable they sound. If you start limiting yourself during this stage of the thinking game, you aren't going to progress very far.

9. Mastermind or accountability partner.

10. Imagine.

What are some ways you will think outside the box to reach your goals?

THE TRUE DEFINITION OF MONEY

MONEY is the root of all miracles.

MONEY can bring huge opportunities.

MONEY gives you the nerve to do what you want and be your truest self.

MONEY is just energy.

MONEY lets you say yes more often to what you want to do, where you want to go and how you want to be.

DREAM = DOING, REACHING, EXUDING, ACTING & MOVING

These are what you need to do bit-by-bit and step-by-step to live your dream. Dare to ask for help, work on yourself, play bold, take action on your dreams, create your own opportunities and jump into them. Most importantly be YOU.

If you had all the MONEY you could imagine, what DREAMS would you pursue?

10+ COMMUNICATIONS, CHOICES & CREATIONS TIPS & AFFIRMATIONS

When you buy amazing flowers and the water turns green and murky, you can dump it out and put in clean clear water; just like when there are things in your life that are murky, you can choose to refresh and clean them.

You know the great feeling in the beginning of a relationship, when you buy a new shirt, get a new pet, new car or begin a dream career? Keep those feelings of love and excitement by remembering to amp it up, appreciate and be amazed at your life.

Self + Acceptance of Self + Awareness of True Self = Self-Love

When you work, find ways to express your soul.

Follow your heart to fulfillment.

Live like dogs by just being LOVE!

Amazing manifestations of what you want can come to you with the proper positive actions!

REMINDER: It takes the same energy to be positive and enthusiastic as it does negative and disempowering. Which do you choose?

Positive people, experiences and opportunities flow to me easily and effortlessly.

Start today with being in the NOW. Notice the beauty, people, things and experiences in your life. Open your eyes, mind and soul to the energy and possibilities. Marvel at your life, being in awe of all of the gifts, both big and small.

Fill up your bucket with smiles, adventures, meaning, creativity and experiences that get you choked up in a good way; meaning, positivity, illuminating beauty, nature, powerful people that inspire you, miracles, gifts, gratitude and sunshine.

Sometimes we just need an interruption to stop a bad mood, off day or low energy. Do jumping jacks; sing out loud, scream or splash water on your face. You'll come out of it and start over!

Gracious, Grateful and Growing = Greatness

Even if you initially do not believe the things you are telling yourself, your mind will absorb it and eventually believe it. I know this sounds a bit odd, but think about it. You have believed you are not good enough only because you have chosen to believe this story. Turn it around! Tell yourself a new story, that you are powerful, strong and undefeatable. This will result in enormous positive changes and opportunities in your life. The first step is to believe you can get your life to a 10+. If you don't believe in yourself and your capabilities, it cannot happen.

Integrity is so huge and important in business and life. Do what you say you'll do, give people more than they pay for and they'll love you, walk the walk, talk the talk and be kind and authentic and you'll go far. This makes you significant, a person of influence with a grand reputation.

Give change and new chapters a hug and allow them to challenge you. They have new exciting gifts for you that can amp up your life in magical ways.

Pow! Boom! Zoom! Zap! Zing! Pop!

The Fourth of July or any holiday where you see or use fireworks is all about excitement, thrills, celebrations and smiles. Take the time this day to be in the moment. Appreciate each memory, laugh a lot and see the wonders of your experiences as you watch each firework rocket to the sky. Use this as a metaphor for your life and dreams soaring to heights that you know deep inside your heart are already a reality. Like a sparkler shining and dripping flames all around, let your truest self and power illuminate the people, places and world.

Cherish your loved ones and friends by lifting them up. Be grateful for those who love you. It's more people than you realize.

ABOUT THE AUTHOR

KIM SOMERS EGELSEE specializes in helping people get every area of their lives to a 10+, exude confidence, connect authentically and discover their life's purpose. She's the #1 bestselling author of *Getting Your Life to a 10 Plus*, and has co-authored eight books, including several in the *Sexy, Fit & Fab* series. Kim is a multi award-winning confidence expert, TEDx speaker, international inspirational speaker, life and business coach, image consultant, hypnotherapist, NLP practitioner, TV host, author and columnist. She speaks at hundreds of events, meetings and workshops per year, and has shared stages with Darren Hardy, Brian Tracy, Dennis Waitley and more. She has reached millions with her message. Kim also certifies people as life coaches in her 10+ Life Coaching Certification Program and Image Consultant Certification Program. Kim works closely with Kyle Wilson (Jim Rohn Int, Your Success Store.com) and Lessons.

LET'S CONNECT!

f y 🅾 g+

Facebook.com/TenPlusConfidence

@KimSomers

@KimLifeCoach

www.KimLifeCoach.com

www.KimsConfidenceCourse.com

KIM SOMERS EGELSEE'S
10 WEEKS TO CONFIDENCE
HOW TO EXUDE CONFIDENCE IN EVERY INTERACTION

Receive a 2 Week All Access Trial to 10 Weeks to Confidence For Only $11.96

Go to 10WeekstoConfidenceTrial.com

- **Week One** – Living A Congruently Confident Life
- **Week Two** – Creating Confident Communication, States, Beliefs and Behaviors
- **Week Three** – Confidence Is Being in Alignment With What You Love
- **Week Four** – Move Forward With Bold Fearlessness
- **Week Five** – Making Space For Greatness
- **Week Six** – Connect And Collaborate For Confidence
- **Week Seven** – Embrace Your Uniqueness
- **Week Eight** – Believe And Achieve Your Power Goals
- **Week Nine** – Ask For What You Want
- **Week Ten** – Bring Your Confidence To The Table And Own It Every Time

Plus Receive 20 Powerful World-Class Confidence and Success Interviews!

10WeekstoConfidenceTrial.com

LIVE IN YOUR FULL POSITIVE POWER!

GETTING YOUR LIFE TO A 10+ PLUS
Tips and Tools for Finding Your Purpose, Being in Your Power and Living an Amazing Life
KIM SOMERS EGELSEE

Tips and Tools for finding your purpose, being in your power and living an amazing life! A powerful how-to book for anyone wanting more happiness, success, and balance in their life. This book gives you the wisdom, stories, and exercises that guide you into self-exploration and positive powerful ways to change your life right away.

LIVING THE 10+ PLUS LIFE
Affirmations, Tips and Activities for Increased Confidence and Success
KIM SOMERS EGELSEE

Are you ready to exude confidence in every aspect of your life? Affirmations, Tips and Activities for increased confidence and success will add bold energy to your life! Create your own opportunities and jump into them, ask for what you want, take action, and live a spectacular *10+ Life!* Amp up your confidence today!

Made in the USA
Columbia, SC
18 November 2024